SEO CHECKLIST (2021)

NOTHING IS COMPLETE UNTILL YOU HAVE A CHECKLIST

ANUJ BHARADWAJ

This Book is dedicated to People Relate to SEO Industry.

Very soon SEO Industry will cross 80 million Dollars So I pray for your happyful future career

in SEO Industry.

Contents

Foreword

This is a SEO checklist for year 2021. If any SEO person impliment this checklist then his Ranking in Search engine will be higher as Compare to his own staregies only.In other words you may say that this is a framework for SEO in 2021.

Preface

This checklist is written to Help SEO people to make sure they are not missing anything
during their regular work. so that they shall not miss the special points to be kept in mind.

ONE

<u>SEO Checklist (2021)</u>

1. **Create keyword on keyword rich content.**

Meaning of Keyword Rich content is Keyword on which ranks for multiple keywords ,you shall select that keyword ,and you shall use secondary keyword as well in your content.

2. **Auto Update your content on monthly Basis using Rankmath plugin**

You can Auto update your content using Rankmath plugin.
You just need to put current month and date in your heading
with help of this plugin and it will auto update your content
on monthly Basis without any effort.

3. **Create long form i.e complete content with FAQ, Images, Videos, GIFs**

Long form content means content which shall give complete information to the reader so

That reader shall not move to any other website for any further information.

Your content must have 3000+ words it will help you in ranking.

Secondly FAQ section has become very important after new update of Google's Algorithm.

Websites having Images ,Videos, GIFs etc helps in ranking as it create customer more engaging.

4. Improve your CTR(using good title, Brackets)

CTR/click through rate is very very important in SEO industry .

If someone ask me for the first thing on which we shall focus

I will suggest the first thing to be kept in focus is CTR

using copywriting in Headline, Bracket or any other possible way you have.

5. Must have SSL certificate Installed.

Many times you saw any website having https:// in the Beginning it means SSL certificate is

Installed in that website. This is not only important for SEO purpose but also security of

Your own website.

6. Link Building with Strategy

We must Build Link with Proper strategy. If you create 10 links on first month then create 10 link on second month also.

You shall create 70 % do follow and 30% no follow link.

7. Build social Presence(VVI)

Social Presence and social signals are very important for ranking as it give trust to Google.
You shall create and link social Presence of your website or Business.

8. Use Voice SEO

Voice SEO is the process when you speak anything to Google and it shows result this is due to voice SEO.

9. Take care of BERT and EAT updates of Google

These are two new updates of Google Algorithm. Please take care of BERT update because it is very
Very Important and Big update.

10. Use more Videos in content(2-3 videos)

Please keep two to three videos in your content because some people like video
And some people like written content. So it will help to improve UI and hence helps
in Ranking.

11. Major Earning which Google gets is from Ads so Google focuses on improving User

Experience. This is shall be kept in mind always and every time to keep ranking for long time.

Bonus : https://drive.google.com/drive/folders/1wB_inU6W1EZ2Hx4IcZJBotwMO8A59YSv?usp=sharing

Youtube channel : https://www.youtube.com/channel/UCVziu27gO3r6gZHstqa-Hzw

Recommended SEO Tool: SEMrush

Affiliate Link For SEMrush : Try https://www.semrush.com/lp/sem/en/?ref=0806004900&utm_campaign=aio_campaign&utm_source=berush&utm_medium=promo&utm_term=23

Sign Up for 7 Day free Trail